A Trickle of Bloom Becomes You

A Trickle of Bloom Becomes You

Jen Rouse

Finalist for the Charlotte Mew Prize

Headmistress Press

Copyright © 2022 by Jen Rouse
All rights reserved.

ISBN 978-1-7358236-8-3

This book may not be reproduced, in whole or in part, including illustrations, in any form (beyond that permitted by Sections 107 and 108 of the U.S. Copyright Law and except by reviewers for the public press), without written permission from the publishers.

Cover art: Frederic Leighton, Flaming June. 1895. Public Domain.

"These 'Queer Flowers'" appeared in HAD.

PUBLISHER
Headmistress Press
60 Shipview Lane
Sequim, WA 98382
Telephone: 917-428-8312
Email: headmistresspress@gmail.com
Website: headmistresspress.blogspot.com

For Eve

Table of Contents

Pteridomania	1
In the Secret Garden	3
A Fairy Spot of Ground	5
A Lengthy Performance	6
Variations	7
Sara Plummer Lemmon, Botanist	8
Of Monsters. Of Plants.	9
Nigella damascena 'Miss Jekyll'	10
Curator of Mosses	11
Mimosa Pudica	12
Wallpaper	13
No. Really. Not Everything is a Man-Eating Vagina, She Said, to the 19th-Century Male Botanist	14
Sundew	15
The Botanist to the Florist	16
By a Friend to Youth	17
These 'Queer Flowers'	18
Transportation of Plants	20
Solanum Baretiae	21
J.M. Cameron Befriends M. North	22
When the Wollstonecraft Women Come Out to Play	23
Your Moral Garden	26
Cells	27
Herbarium	28
Good Student of the Earth	29
Selenicereus Grandiflorus	30
To Grow a Monster	31
Approaching Death like a Botanist	32
About the Author	33

Pteridomania[1]

Observe. Meaning: the first
to notice. Where a foot
softly falls. A skirt drifts
to forest floor. How removed
are we from the word
discovery? They will call
this madness. When a
woman collects, classifies,
succumbs to science.

They said: *but ferns
are safer than novels
and gossip.*[2] Until they
weren't. Until, of course,
the hysteria began. Because
doesn't it always begin
when they give us something
to do? And, perhaps, we're
good at it? To be kept
in your Wardian cases[3] or
to be keepers of our own
selves? Press, dry the maiden
hair, the curly-grass. Watch
as the fiddlehead unfurls
to the touch. Send your social
reformers out to find our
spores, light in the air. Pray
we never touch down—try
as you might to catch us,
here in the mist, evolving.

---

[1] Fern mania in the Victorian era. The term 'pteridomania' was

coined in 1855 by Charles Kingsley in his book *Glaucus, or the Wonders of the Shore.*
[2] Atributed to Kingsley.
[3] Wardian cases were created by Nathaniel Bagshaw Ward in 1892. They were tightly-sealed glass cases for growing ferns. Much like a terrarium.

In the Secret Garden

When the botanists &
poets[4] come to tea, they
trade monogamy for
illicit gossip of poppies—
wanton, Darwinian.[5]

Allowed to document
the flowers, they crack
wise about their new
language, lush and
unencumbered. Linnaeus,[6]
god of plant sex, how
they worship at your
salty altar. Lick at the
edge of order. Paint
in oils. Formidable.

For this unwatched
moment, even the wind
is promiscuous. Notes are
furious in the margins. To
document the undone. And
so they choose their forest
suitors. Without blush
or proper etiquette.

---

[4] Anna Seward (1742-1809), poet closely connected to the Lichfield Botanical Society, including Erasmus Darwin, who saw the necessity of writing about the sexuality of botany, but maintained that it was "not strictly proper for a female pen."

[5] Erasmus Darwin (1731-1802), renowned for his long poems that overtly explored sex and science. Enlightenment reformer. Inspiring

grandfather to Charles.
[6] Carl Linnaeus, known as the "father of taxonomy." In 1753, published what is considered a starting point of modern botanical nomenclature, the *Species Plantarum*.

A Fairy Spot of Ground[7]

Perhaps the way this garden
plays in light and shadow, in
slurping fountain majesty, in
clandestine benches tucked
into cascading foliage, in the
night blooming jasmine scent
that masks all others,
   Perhaps the way this garden
turns its pale petals to the nape
of your neck, its nestling mosses
against your breast, its elegant
fortress hedges behind your
supple spine,
   Perhaps the way this garden
lingers in divine memory, in
the softly hanging jewels of
bleeding hearts, in the body
you are so certain bends its
silhouette out of the mist,
   this garden so designed you
for every breathless bloom
and its suspense.

---

[7] Mary Granville Pendarves Delany (1700-1788), famous for botanical illustrations, often referred to her garden design work as a way to create "fairy spots," her ideal place for female friendships to take place.

A Lengthy Performance[8]

Bring me the tide and the sky,
delicate feathers of the sea,
each winged alga suspended
in Prussian blue. Iron and sun
memory-carve you.

Here is the divine light
where art and science
meet. Not to create a
likeness but to capture
in contour the vibrant
life itself. Symbiotic.
Cyanotyped.[9] Your sorted
gentle cells. Sewn image
to text, a woman might see.
Beyond words. To bring
you this choir of many.

---

[8] From a letter botanist and photographer Anna Atkins (1799-1871) wrote to a friend, describing Atkins' work of creating cyanotypes of over 400 British algae for what is considered the first book to be illustrated with photographs, entitled *Photographs of British Algae: Cyanotype Impressions* (1843).

[9] The cyanotype technique (or blueprint process) was created by Sir John Herschel—a family friend to Atkins. Atkins popularized the technique which involves using iron compounds in conjunction with UV light. The image remains white where the object blocks the light. When the coated paper is washed with water, it oxidizes and creates the cyan-blue contour.

Variations

Actions of other
organisms might
mis/shape you.
Turning one tender
head of rhodo-
dendron to sturdy
shrub. Fire in
design and conse-
quence. Borders
beget trumpeting
wildness. In varia-
tion. Your genes
split and shatter
against. The perfect
pattern for china.
To adapt in ponticum
purple. You are
stripped of crown,
with the hiss of
invasive at your
heels. Only in the
garden is there such
certainty in dis/order.

Sara Plummer Lemmon, Botanist[10]

Substantial leather. Firm
calfskin shoes. A broad
brimmed hat with buckskin
mask. Fortunately, they
bothered to mention a botanical
folio. But that came far below
their concern I might be taken
by snake or cacti from the
terrible mountain. Santa Catalina.
Tuscon from above. Not to
pillage but to document. "J.G.
Lemmon and Wife." How many
times was I *Wife?* The rare
woman in "short suit of strong
material." A golden poppy.
California sunlight. See me now.
A cup of shine. And brilliance.

---

[10] Sara Allen Plummer (1836-1923) was an American botanist. Her work kept her primarily in California and Arizona, where Mount Lemmon is named for her. She devoted considerable energy to writing the bill that would name the golden poppy as California's state flower in 1903.

OF MONSTERS. OF PLANTS.

She dreams each night that her arm extends into the shape of a lily. The scent reminiscent of hours spent in her grandmother's garden. The color extraordinary like the poisonous purple sister flower in *Rapaccinni's Daughter*. Her mind is Hawthorneian. But Edgar's heart beats in the floorboards. Or in the lily pulsing where her fingers should be. The scent sounds like a fluttering heart. When she sears her lily hand to yours, a trickle of bloom becomes you. In that moment that extends between worlds, a choice must be made. Or has it been made in the floorboards. Where you are certain you have met each night. Her scent like lilies beating time in your dream. When you wake what kind of hand are you holding?

Nigella damascena 'Miss Jekyll'[11]

Here the hardy, the devil-in-a-bush,
the bird's nest, the garden fennel.
You call on Turner[12] for a cacophony
of drama and spectacle of color.
Self-splitting from plant to brush to
drift, a border to kiss the edge
of the wild. To love one you must
know both. Love-in-a-puzzle. Kiss-
me-twice-before-I-rise. Fill my eye
with strong reds and desirous
yellows so "grey and glaucous
foliate looks strangely cool and
clear."[13] Know your ghosts by
your darlings. Love-in-a-mist,
jack-in-prison. Your father calls
you a "queer fish,"[14] but you are
Nigella damascena. Miss Jekyll
Dark Blue. Miss Jekyll of the
saturated geometry. To be right
"from all points, and in all lights."[15]

---

[11] Gertrude Jekyll (1843-1932), artist and writer, known for designing hundreds of Victorian gardens, bred a handful of hardy plants to sustain them, including *Nigella damascene* 'Miss Jekyll Dark Blue.

[12] Jekyll was encouraged to study JMW Turner at the National School of Art in South Kensington.

[13] Jekyll G. 1925. Colour schemes for the flower garden, 6th ed. *Country Life*.

[14] "Great British garden-makers: Gertrude Jekyll." *Country Life*, January 23, 2010.

[15] Jekyll, *Wood and Garden*, 156–7.

Curator of Mosses[16]

To split and split
again the small
hands of water.
A kaleidoscope of green
stars: *Polytrichum*[17]
to root. She dreams
of all the ways air
might move through
and against, sputtering
to life in front of her
lens. Listen. What silences
itself in winter will
call out like a spring
mistress. 170 times she
will name you *bryophyte*—
constant embryo of the
ground. She will claim
you as her very own
xeromorph. Hush now.
Evergreen. Unbranched.
Slide into the sandy
forest floor with all
your fingers. Breathe.

---

[16] Elizabeth Gertrude Knight Britton (1857-1934) wrote 170 papers on mosses. She was a renowned bryologist and one of the co-founders of the New York Botanical Garden, where she was an honorary Curator of Mosses.

[17] "Polytrichum (also known as common haircap, great golden maidenhair, great goldilocks, common haircap moss, or common hair moss) is a species of moss found in many regions with high humidity and rainfall." In Edwards, Sean R. (2012). *English Names for British Bryophytes*. British Bryological Society Special Volume. 5 (4 ed.). Wootton, Northampton: British Bryological Society.

Mimosa Pudica

What if your only language was shame,
and that made you a curiosity? And what
if what they thought was shame was also
electricity? And what if the laws of physics
were really always poems to begin with?
When the only option is to turn away,
fold each leaf up in explosive unison. You
are nyctinastic! Hold your breath and let
all cells fire into the darkness. Know hope
in the smallest droplet of water. If we call
this a defense to keep the beasts at bay—
are you mechanical or vital? What if you
were always beautiful but no one told you?
Instead they inflicted. Called you names.
Sensitive. And defined themselves as not.
How you always moved their small thinking
forward. Humble plant. Fighting into light.

WALLPAPER

Let's all make a pact to keep women away from wallpaper. Whether it writhes in mirrored yellow figures, or traps one's brain in a collective mushroom consciousness of evil. Even if you really love ferns and want them everywhere. Avoid the wallpaper. I give you this permission for the rest of our time here. Gather what you can. Seeds you've saved through winter heartbreak. Bulbs from the first house where you remember peace or passion. Your grandmother's lily-of-the-valley cheering you on. Walk away from the wallpaper. Split new earth open with all you have. Take notes for the hands that will follow your hands. Plant and press and paint. Study each cell for a better day. Look carefully for the plants that will sustain you. Never let them name you mad.

No. Really. Not Everything is a Man-Eating Vagina, She Said, to the 19th-Century Male Botanist

Because how could something
dare defy classification and
not be terrifying? Not be other?
Not take the shape of what you covet
and want to control? Insectivores.
You sit in your overstuffed
colonizer suit and remark upon
the irritability of leaves. How can
a plant make you prey? The swamp
sweat clings to your brow. Your palms
tremble to touch the milky hairs
of the mouth, once more. In letters
to your bros, you are predictable,
predatory. You call the carnivorous
by a name too ugly to eat. It
taunts you with some showy
blooms. They are selective and
tiny goddesses mock you, whisper,
come closer. You use your best
schoolboy Latin: *Dionaea muscipula.*
It doesn't matter. So much
of you is already missing, and
you will never make it home.

SUNDEW[18]

First, be smart about the slaughter.
You are pretty in pink, shiny and
slick in the middle. All the moths
and butterflies adore you. I watch
as they become fertilizer at your
feet. But it's your mouth really,
full of dew and so desirous—
You quietly fold around small
bits of beef. Aware that I am
courting your attention. Each delicate
hair aquiver when I place a fly
near. I will observe your short-
term memory glow before me, and
call it sensitivity. To digest.

So alike, we two.
Even Darwin
will take notice.

---

[18] Mary Lua Adelia Davis Treat (1830–1923) made great contributions to the field of botany. She was also known for her work as a naturalist, entomologist, and author. She had over a five-year correspondence with Charles Darwin, discussing, primarily, their studies of carnivorous plants.

The Botanist to the Florist

British soil knows
best, especially in
death, such funerary
virtue. The broken lily
on her urn, snowdrops and
a nation at her feet. So
much to be said in a
grave's white blanket.

Never turn tulip (shhhhh
trollop) or buy the flowers
yourself. Debauchery is
a ranunculus kiss, in the
raining hands of a delicate
florist. We are not, and will

never be, exotic foreign
words unsovereign. We
fill our beds with sturdy
stock. Hide our secrets
in the hedgerows.

By a Friend to Youth[19]

first they will
make you small
in a time when
holding the sky
is precarious at best
and unavailable
if you are wrong.
you will always
be wife before
winner. a professional
amateur. so start your
studies of Wakefield
while you can, and
if we are "pleasant
and familiar" let that be
understood as capable
and determined. how
will you choose to break
open to evolution?
spark to spore to cell
and photosynthesis.
turn a lily to the lens,
slip from field to forest
like a moleculed
goddess. and begin.

---

[19] Sarah Hoare (1777-1856) was a British poet and artist known for her scientific poetry. Her "A Poem on the Pleasures and Advantages of Botanical Pursuits" was included in one of the first botany texts written by a woman. That text was Priscilla Wakefield's *An Introduction to Botany, in a Series of Familiar Letters,* London, 1796. Hoare's poem also appears in a collection of her own work with no author listed. Instead it is said to be written "By a Friend to Youth, Addressed to Her Pupils."

These 'Queer Flowers'[20]

Because plants
are not proper.
We know them
to be messy and loud
and riotous in
color. Holding
tightly to their
stories. Unna-
med—the fertile
fingers of the
first finders,
the doctress-
es, the healers
who knew them
well before the
spectacle. Unfold-
ed. Perfect for the
Gothic. In their
'Murderous prop-
ensities.' Place
your man-
eating tree
smack in the middle
of your haunted
mansion. Begui-
ling. The way
the undead
beckon. With
evolution on
their breath and
the promise
of a woman.

[20] Grant Allen (1848-1899), Canadian science writer and novelist, described insectivorous plants as "queer flowers," "floral femme fatales" with "murderous propensities." In Smith, Jonathan. "Une fleur du mal? Swinburne's 'The Sundew' and Darwin's Insectivorous Plants." *Victorian Poetry* vol. 41 no. 1, 2003, p. 131-150.

Transportation of Plants

To get the snapping jawed
across the Atlantic. To fill
the salons. Kew clamored.
To flourish without care
in a curious case. Kept
from sea air and mercurial
climates. What would they
do to discover you? A frenzy
for the feeding. To own
just a moment. Of pure
spectacle. To believe
you were created just
for their pleasure. Open
wide. Destroy the new
world order. And then some.

Solanum Baretiae[21]

Imagine a ship named star
and a vine you will eventually
claim as bougainvillea,
the captain who keeps you on
in your slight disguise. Your fuck boy
who can't quite live without you,
calling you his beast of burden.
You unburden yourself of children.
Replace them with plants.
To circumnavigate the globe of
desires. Beyond the rule book
for women. Which you refuse
to read. Sail on. We name you
nightshade that sounds of sun
from all your travels. Somewhere
in Port-Louis pouring out
liquor on Sundays. You tip
your cap, wipe down the bar.

---

[21] A nightshade named in honor of Jeanne Baret, a botanist who disguised herself as a man to sail as the assistant to botanist Philibert Commerson on Louis Antoine de Bougainville's global circumnavigation (1766–1769). Women were not allowed on French naval vessels during this time.

J.M. Cameron[22] Befriends M. North[23]

On the day she wears the green
shawl, I am certain marriage is
still not for me. "Yes, that would
just suit you," she fusses, having
split the fabric into something shared.

I want you to know
I leave everything
where it belongs.

Nepenthes northiana named my
name. From the limestone mountains.
Borneo. The light opens wide to
this new pitcher plant. It sings
on my canvas its full-throated
bass. My only place, here,
is inside the landscape.

Where she drapes me with
this ornamental sun. Beautiful
Julia. Don't we always stage the
natural? Order the sublime.
She takes down my braids.
And I become her virgin
Mary of the coconut palm.

---

[22] Julia Margaret Cameron (18150-1879). A British photographer of soft-focus, primarily allegorical, close-up portraiture. All original, and sometimes contentious, techniques for this time.

[23] Marianne North (1830-1890). North made many plant discoveries as a biologist and botanical artist travelling the world. Her inherited wealth allowed her much freedom in her travels and work, and she commissioned her own gallery at the Royal Botanic Gardens, Kew.

Wollstonecraft Women Come Out to Play

I.
Ignore the sleepy poppy and
Rousseau. Salvation slips in through
the pulse of a tulip. Be there
with purpose and chlorophyll
on your thumb. You are not exotic.
So cultivate a different strain
of beauty. Rip out the delicate
flower and her luxurious decay.
Dear sister, they will think to
rediscover you centuries later,
anyway. So live. Keep Linnaeus
in your pocket and Wakefield
as a bible. Shall we? Ignore
the sleepy poppy, and instead
suckle our daughters on science?

II.
Though she never
says to mother is to
be white with white
daughters, M. encourages
only their botanical
leanings, looks past
the hands that plant
survival gardens from
seed, body and blood
embedded. The woman-
slave rhetoric persists.
This thick Protestant
discourse. Not the vindi-

cation of all women
but those who break free.
The imperative emerging
from action. From a morals-
soaked narrative, she will
call herself abolitionist.
She will be wrong.

III.
Anne Kingsbury Wollstonecraft

At the edge of my life,
I will board the boat.
To convalesce, they
said, the Wollstonecrafts
who talk of Cuba. And
send me on my way.

The record of my work,
not my supposed infirmity,
will rise again, 190 years
later. Voluminous. Layered,
this botanical cake of poetry,
plant, and paint. To be lost

perhaps is just to listen. To
the most important voices
of the past. They say, take
up watercolors. It's peaceful.
I resist this diminished

chord and its smaller song
of myself. There is such a large
voice in Mantanzas. The language
of healing when so many have

arrived deeply wounded. Yes,

I listen and record each pronunciation,
capture elixirs and compounds,
emerging from bark and root,
frond and fern. Paint the process
of the living. A manuscript

of citrus scent, setting here.
An angel's trumpet. To return.

Your Moral Garden

Sin and thorn, keep your
hybrid thinking tight
in your throat. Flutter
a handkerchief if
anyone gets too close
to your deep knowledge.
They will come for
the tulips first, the wild
life of the pansy, the flirty
fronds, the contraband.
Insatiable for insect-
catchers. We are one
Freud closer to the
criminal mind. The cruel
indifference. The angst
of a poppy. The heartache
carnation. Whatever has
been hidden will rise
again. Grand Design be
damned. So instruct with
a bouquet of purple violets—
so much lies in the tie
of the knot, the choice of
delivering hand.

Cells

I was the kind of child who loved drawing the beauty of science. I might've been a perfect Victorian lady of plant painting. It's true. Except, maybe, for the well-coiffed part. The neatness. Perhaps moral precision would've been my downfall. Hard to tell. Definitely of the having-one-very-good-woman-friend variety. Tough and up to the conversations of men. All this if the asylum hadn't nicked me. But, even then, so many gardens to paint. I should probably tell you that I've never kept a plant alive. And for 30 years my brain tried to kill me every day. The skeleton cactus on my windowsill is proof. I remember making a plant cell when I was young. Out of a genoise sponge. It was turn-your-teeth green, a bright springy cake that looked as lovely as its name and the sounds of science: mitochondria, membrane, reticulum. I'm not sure I ever really made meaning of any of it. So many extraordinary ways to enter and exit the light.

Herbarium

So close   you press
each leaf   light the page with
intimate knowledge   this place
no matter   your marriage or   its absence
your children   or their   deliverance
this ground   grows you   home
you will fall through people   but
the forest flora   will restore you
settle order   through the seeded stars   book upon
book you carefully weigh   and measure
what history will hold
                        and hold you back
to know where you are   and what held
you there   to gather together
each detail   a petal a pod as perfect
as something collected can be
to share the system   divinely
secured   and so cemented   unbruised
in centuries   turn to the hill   bring
only what you can carry   need

Good Student of the Earth

It seems I have always been quiet—and here, even in the roar and squander of the city, I have listened. I have become. These hands. Here we are now. With only these hands. Undulating fields of fierce and soothing herbs, a kind of language shared between us. Healing the wounded and broken in the thick and humid mist, with the tenderness of breath and touch. And you would've thought I might've added god there. To the list of what is needed. But god is what is given. It is what you do with your piece of the given that matters.

How did you hold that sliver under your tongue? In what shape and shadow? In what silver moon and sun and beaded fortune? Were you a good student of the earth? And did you hold her face to the splendor of the last light?

I have lived the question. With each turned leaf and mortared root. Where in the body does your god take hold? Where is the poison of regret? Listen to the blood song, the delicate balance of plant and raindrop. How it thrums in your chest.

And when you have slept all night in the desert, when you have given everything to the hive, when you have cradled the last remaining bits of your sanity and asked only for an end, look once more for a teacher. I promise. Someone else will come.

Selenicereus Grandiflorus

Root-entombed, a Queen who listens
to lamented day and courts the moon.
Encanto. You are legend to Tohono
O'odham. Old-Mother-White-Head,
there to remind of faith as fragrant
as your bloom. The vanilla-scented
desert opens out from you. We answer
when our daughters call.   To white men,
you were immediately a mystery. A hypnotic
riddle. A trick-of-the-night virgin to
undo. Cerea! they called you, stung
and outwitted. Never to sleep, but to call
your ghosts, slip them through the veil.
The slight touch of bat wing. Hawk moths
at your open throat. Complete and opalescent.

To Grow a Monster

A clandestine marriage. A bit
of Cryptogamia. How a vegetable
and animal make "histories of
a marvelous kind."[24] Some will
story you birthed a lamb
-like god, in full golden fleece,
creeping across a faraway land,
feasting. To be flayed and furred
for royal shoulders. Others conquest
and find you succulent. Stripping
you flesh from stalk. Gothic against
a nation's wealth. Are you fern
or cotton? A terrible lamb shaped
by whose hands? And for what
purpose? Let your yellow down
protect you. Rise small root, through
the monster of empire. Rustle small
fern, fable and all.

---

[24] Maria Jacson's description of a tartarian lamb in her *Botanical Lectures by a Lady* (1804).

Approaching Death like a Botanist

Finger to finger with lake-
suckled cedar. Chewing the
spicy needle of a giant
pine. Would you feather
into the frond of a fern?
Or make your final bed
against a blanket of
mosses? To return again
to discovery. Wondering
what you will grow with
your best cells shed? How
else to greet fear but by
waiting for the ghost of
a birch to walk you from
this place. You remember
her best, dressed as she
always is in her trailing
gown of cloudy skin. Take the
hem of her. To the edge
of every forest. Tell the most
beautiful story of something
risen from ash and loam.

About the Author

Jen Rouse directs the Center for Teaching and Learning at Cornell College. Her work has appeared in *Lavender Review, SWWIM, Sinister Wisdom, Pithead Chapel, Mississippi Review,* and elsewhere. She lives in Iowa City with her wife, daughter, and two rambunctious wheaten terriers, Sunny & Snowy.

Headmistress Press Books

Tender, Tender - Jessica Jewell
A Trickle of Bloom Becomes You - Jen Rouse
Cyborg Sister - Jackie Craven
Demoted Planet - Katherine Fallon
Earlier Households - Bonnie J. Morris
The Things We Bring with Us: Travel Poems - S.G. Huerta
The Water Between Us - Gillian Ebersole
Discomfort - Sarah Caulfield
The History of a Voice - Jessica Jopp
I Wish My Father - Lesléa Newman
Tender Age - Luiza Flynn-Goodlett
Low-water's Edge - Jean A. Kingsley
Routine Bloodwork - Colleen McKee
Queer Hagiographies - Audra Puchalski
Why I Never Finished My Dissertation - Laura Foley
The Princess of Pain - Carolyn Gage & Sudie Rakusin
Seed - Janice Gould
Riding with Anne Sexton - Jen Rouse
Spoiled Meat - Nicole Santalucia
Cake - Jen Rouse
The Salt and the Song - Virginia Petrucci
mad girl's crush tweet - summer jade leavitt
Saturn coming out of its Retrograde - Briana Roldan
i am this girl - gina marie bernard
Week/End - Sarah Duncan
My Girl's Green Jacket - Mary Meriam
Nuts in Nutland - Mary Meriam & Hannah Barrett
Lovely - Lesléa Newman
Teeth & Teeth - Robin Reagler
How Distant the City - Freesia McKee
Shopgirls - Marissa Higgins
Riddle - Diane Fortney
When She Woke She Was an Open Field - Hilary Brown

A Crown of Violets - Renée Vivien tr. Samantha Pious
Fireworks in the Graveyard - Joy Ladin
Social Dance - Carolyn Boll
The Force of Gratitude - Janice Gould
Spine - Sarah Caulfield
I Wore the Only Garden I've Ever Grown - Kathryn Leland
Diatribe from the Library - Farrell Greenwald Brenner
Blind Girl Grunt - Constance Merritt
Acid and Tender - Jen Rouse
Beautiful Machinery - Wendy DeGroat
Odd Mercy - Gail Thomas
The Great Scissor Hunt - Jessica K. Hylton
A Bracelet of Honeybees - Lynn Strongin
Whirlwind @ Lesbos - Risa Denenberg
The Body's Alphabet - Ann Tweedy
First name Barbie last name Doll - Maureen Bocka
Heaven to Me - Abe Louise Young
Sticky - Carter Steinmann
Tiger Laughs When You Push - Ruth Lehrer
Night Ringing - Laura Foley
Paper Cranes - Dinah Dietrich
On Loving a Saudi Girl - Carina Yun
The Burn Poems - Lynn Strongin
I Carry My Mother - Lesléa Newman
Distant Music - Joan Annsfire
The Awful Suicidal Swans - Flower Conroy
Joy Street - Laura Foley
Chiaroscuro Kisses - G.L. Morrison
The Lillian Trilogy - Mary Meriam
Lady of the Moon - Amy Lowell, Lillian Faderman, Mary Meriam
Irresistible Sonnets - ed. Mary Meriam
Lavender Review - ed. Mary Meriam

www.ingramcontent.com/pod-product-compliance
Lightning Source LLC
Chambersburg PA
CBHW060223050426
42446CB00013B/3153